BURKITT'S BOOK OF
BAD MOTORCYCLE POETRY

To Father Sergiu

Best wishes

Morgan / the Poet /
Burkitt

BURKITT'S
BOOK
OF
BAD
MOTORCYCLE POETRY

NORMAN BURKITT

Old King Cole Poetry Books
Burkitt's Book of Bad Motorcycle Poetry written by
Norman Burkitt & illustrated by Manfred

Old King Cole Publishing Ltd
Registered Office: 26 Rhodes Court, 5 Jefferson Place, Bromley, BR2 9FY
OLD KING COLE and associated logos are trademarks and/or registered
trademarks of Old King Cole Publishing Ltd

First published by Old King Cole Publishing Ltd 2020
Text and illustrations © Norman Burkitt and Manfred ~
Design edits by Geoff Fisher

ISBN: 978-0-9934496-5-9

A CIP catalogue record for this book is available from the British Library.

Printed and bound in Great Britain by CPI Group (UK) Ltd,
Croydon, CR0 4YY.

okc@gmx.co.uk

FSC
www.fsc.org
MIX
Paper from
responsible sources
FSC® C013604

AKNOWLEDGEMENTS

Eyvor Fogarty for her help and encouragement, Nadine and Jan of Old King Cole Publishing without whom this book would not have been written.

Del (Del Boy) Toomey – good friend sadly missed.

Ben, Sharon Riddle, Yeliz Hakki and Manfred for their artwork. Bruno and Lydia for their support.

Terry Sparks for his encouragement.

Danny Butler, Dave Janes and Mick Abbott. Not forgetting Mark and Linda Wilsmore of the 'Ace Café' for their initial support some twenty years ago.

Dave Mills, Dave Hayes, The Big Seven Scooter Club (Barry).

The Biggin Hill Ton-Up Boys and Rockers, Riders of the 'Goss'. The 'Coppice' Mods, Orpington and Bromley Mods, Peckham Mods (Dave Murray).

Also, Tony Nichols and Frankie Rumble from Daily Express (1962) – they knew me as 'Bill'.

John Cooper Clark (nice chap); met him once in Brixton. Friend of Zita's and Lizzie's (Rob Pearson).

DEDICATION

Mum and Dad, Pete Graves, Dave Fellows, Ken Kirk, Betty, Sharon, Mick, Chris, Sid Speed, his wife and daughter Lucy. Chick, Glenn, Keith Chard, Wally, Pam and all the old crowd. Norm Shigley and Cherry. The great John Humphreys and Kenny Rowlands.

CONTENTS

FOREWORD

'What is good, Phaedrus, and what is not good – need we ask anyone to tell us these things?'

Quote from Robert Persig

THE WILD HALF

I'm a part-time motorcycle hero,
A weekend rebellious tearaway.
I'd like to think that I'm The Wild One,
But I'm more like The Wild Half, as you might say.

In the week I work up in the city.
An office clerk boring nine to five.
When I take me bike out on a Friday night,
It's then that I seem to come alive.

I would like to live in California
Or some large place I haven't tried.
Or ride upon the Trans-Canada highway
With a pack of desperadoes at my side.

You must be thankful for small mercies, though.
At least when we meet up, we have a laugh.
I'm a full-time, part-time biking hero.
The laid-back king of coolness: The Wild Half.

THE ROCKER AND THE ALIEN

The Rocker and the Alien
Stood together on the sand.
Said the Alien to the Rocker
As he took him by the hand:

'I shouldn't be here, really.'
And he said it from the heart,
'I should have left already
But my shuttle wouldn't start.'

'As you're here,' said the Rocker,
'You might help us in our plight.
We've been trying for ages
But we still can't get it right.

There's too much destruction,
Violence and fear.
Tell me, Mr Alien
Can this be why we're here?'

'Ah!' said the Alien
As he looked into the stars.
'Things could be different
If soldiers played guitars.'

'If soldiers played guitars?'
The Rocker looked at him askew.
'If soldiers played guitars,
What would Rock 'n' Rollers do?'

2

'Well, they could get a job, my friend,
They could be like you.'

'Must go,' said the Alien,
'It's nearly half past three.
I only live a light year hence.
Should be back in time for tea.'

One flash; he was out to sea.
Another, up to sky.
The Rocker sat upon his bike.
'Goodbye, old mate. Goodbye.'

'If soldiers played guitars.'
The words whirled round his brain.
'If soldiers played guitars. That's it!
That would end the pain.'

'There's too much destruction,
Violence and fear.
Tell me, Mr Alien,
Can this be why we're here?'

THE MOD WHO NEVER WAS

They found him drifting in the sea;
No clue of his identity;
His clothes were ripped and torn now;
Damaged skin upon his brow.

In his eyes a far-off glaze;
He's been floating there for days.
He'd been floating out of reach;
About a mile from Brighton Beach.

No-one knows him now you see;
In this summer of sixty-three.
No one knows him now because;
He's the Mod that never was.

THE LEGION OF LOST MODS

There is a ghostly battalion
That can be seen from time-to-time,
The Legion of Lost Mods,
Riding down the line.

Coming back from a rumble,
Riding from the coast.
Coming back from a rumble,
Every one of them a ghost.

Ripped and torn parkas,
Blood-stained desert boots,
Their comradeship was strong,
Tightly in cahoots.

Their comradeship was strong,
This cannot be denied,
The Legion of Lost Mods,
Forever they will ride.

THE JOLLY NICE CHAPS'
MOTORCYCLE CLUB

The Jolly Nice Chaps' Motorcycle Club
Are sometimes known as the J.N.C.
They really are a splendid lot.
Those who know them all agree.

The leader Johnny 'Ton-Up' Teddington
[An Oxford educated man]
Works part-time down the village
Where he drives a grocer's van.

They do a lot for charity,
Always helping out.
They have a splendid reputation.
They carry a lot of clout.

They do garage sales for money
In league with the Women's Institute.
When not riding his Interceptor,
'Tiger' Archer plays the flute.

The long-haired commander Summers
Once won the Paris-Dakar race.
To make things a little harder
He wore a grapefruit on his face.

The flexible Freddy Mathews
[A sergeant in the RAF]
Has his bike down at the fairground
Where he rides the Wall of Death.

When you find yourself in trouble
You can always call them out.
They'd really love to help you.
It's what they're all about.

THE FIFTH ASSASSIN

I almost thought I saw him:
The assassin, or one of the assassins.
He was standing on a parapet
Overlooking the Plaza.
He was a cop, or dressed as one.
He was holding a rifle.
At first I thought he was an ordinary cop
Going about his business,
But after the shooting, I felt differently.
I kept my eyes on him
Throughout the ensuing commotion.
I saw him fire the rifle,
Get on his motorcycle,
And move slowly away.

THE BATTERED MOD

Cyril worked in a chip shop
Frying battered cod.

Bad Rockers stole his takings,
Beat him up.
He became the Battered Mod.

They beat him up so badly
He nearly lost his life.

He still lives above the chip shop
With two kids and a wife.

THE CONCRETE ROCKER

He was famous in his town,
He saved a child about to drown.
Johnny Blige A.K.A. the Concrete Rocker.

On his bike seated thus,
Is a man that you can trust.
Johnny Blige A.K.A. the Concrete Rocker.

They made a statue from cement,
The bike was fashioned; heaven sent.
Johnny Blige A.K.A. the Concrete Rocker.

His grandchild now surveys the scene,
He's not quite sure what it all means.
His grandad, Johnny Blige, the Concrete Rocker.

I WISH IT WAS YESTERDAY

I wish it was yesterday.
No matter what you say,
I wish it was yesterday.
Motorcycles by the gate,
It didn't matter if you got home late.

Down at the coffee bar,
Our favourite jukebox recording star,
Billy Fury, Marty Wilde,
Eddie Cochran Rock and Roll style.

No matter what you say,
I wish it was yesterday.
Everybody dressed up cool,
We'd only just left school.

I went out wearing my denim coat
Clutching in my hand a ten-bob note.
Mods on scooters riding past,
Things seemed to be changing fast.

No matter what you say,
I wish it was yesterday.
Motorcycles by the gate,
It didn't matter if you got home late.

YOUNG TURKS

The traditional Turkish Barber shop
Was positioned on the right
When the boys had finished work
They would ride into the night

Young Turks on the Highway
Young Turks riding fast
Young Turks on the Mile End Road
Down the underpass

The bikes were very powerful
The boys kept them nice and clean
They held them all in high regard
They were proud of their machines

Young Turks on the Highway
Young Turks riding fast
Young Turks on the Mile End Road
Down the underpass

The traditional Turkish Barber shop
Was positioned on the right
When the boys had finished work
They would ride into the night

Young Turks

TEDDY BEAR BIKERS

The guitar strikes the chord 'Kerrang'
Here comes the teddy bear biker's gang
The teddy bear bikers are getting all around
Teddy bear bikers are taking over the town
It's not safe, I hear someone say
Don't go down in the woods today
Teddy bear bikers are gathering all around
It's not normal, I can't comprehend
Oh yeah what's normal then my friend?
Teddy bear bikers are gathering all around
Teddy bear bikers are taking over the town
We think of them as cuddly toys
But these ones ain't, they're biker boys
Teddy bear bikers we'd better get away
Teddy bear bikers could be here to stay

LEADER OF THE WHATEVER

His name was John but they called him Jack
He was the leader, the leader of the whatever
His dad saw him from his car
And said 'Look at him, my son's a star'

'He is the leader
The leader of the whatever'

He was cool and he was tall
Very well put together
He was the leader
The leader of the whatever

He looked great on his bike
He looks great as well he might
He looked good in leather
The leader of the whatever

He looked good in leather
The leader of the whatever
Whatever

THOSE LESS ABLE TO STAND

He was a notorious Ton-up boy,
The most daring in the land.
In his spare time though he was
Caring and would always lend a hand
To the disabled
   the pregnant
   and those less able to stand.

He looked tough and was tough,
But he would always lend a hand
To the disabled
   the pregnant
   and those less able to stand.

His pals said, 'You're wasting your time, mate.'
But they didn't understand.
He answered in a friendly way,
'It never hurts to lend a hand.'

In his spare time though he was
Caring and would always lend a hand
To the disabled
   the pregnant
   and those less able to stand.

ROGUE MALE

Wrong guy, wrong place, wrong time
He doesn't really fit in anywhere
Wrong guy, wrong place, wrong time
He wouldn't have it any other way
Another tank of gas and he's on his way
Rogue male
Vaya con dios

ARMAGEDDON OUT OF HERE

Buildings are cracking
I see the blackened sun
Water mains are bursting
Where can we run?

I've got my bike piled high
With survival gear
If this is Armageddon
Armageddon out of here

ZOMBIE MODS

What's happening here ye gods?
We're being attacked by zombie Mods
Zombie Mods are coming into town

Women scream, can't blame 'em much
They would tremble at the touch
Tremble at the touch of
                          zombie Mods

A lot is being left unsaid
Zombie Mods are quite undead
Here's a bunch of zombie Mods
With clothes in rags and a growling sound
These boys are tearing up the ground
There is no escape from
                          zombie Mods

Police sirens wail to no avail
It's no good putting them in jail
What are we gonna do about
                          zombie Mods?

People get down on their knees
They don't wanna catch this zom disease
They don't wanna be undead like
                          zombie Mods

There is a terrible plot a hatchin'
What these boys have must be catchin'
Lord help us stay away from
zombie Mods

THIRTY DUSTMEN

Thirty dustmen came riding
Riding for their rights
Thirty dustmen came riding
On big and heavy bikes
Thirty dustmen came riding
Riding for their rights
Thirty dustmen came riding

Thirty dustmen came riding
Riding for their rights
Riding three long days and three long nights
Thirty dustmen came riding
Riding for their rights
Thirty dustmen came riding

Thirty dustmen came riding
Riding for their rights
Wearing sling-back hobnailed boots
    and sequinned lurex tights
Thirty dustmen came riding
Riding for their rights
Thirty dustmen came riding

They handed their petition to the man
    behind the plate
They handed their petition before it was too late
Thirty dustmen came riding
Riding to the gate
Thirty dustmen came riding riding riding
Thirty dustmen

VINCENT OWNER AT THE BIKE MEET

He was a Vincent owner
Nothing wrong with that
But when you went to talk to him
He made you feel a pratt
He'd obviously come along here
To show off his smashing bike
But he was rude and arrogant
Maybe it was people he didn't like
He was a Vincent owner
One of the best bikes ever made
But the owner's personality
Put the bike in the shade
Vincent owner at the bike meet

CAPRILLO AND MUSKRATT

Caprillo and Muskratt
Were running from the law
Caprillo and Muskratt
Had done this sort of thing before
They'd robbed a bank in Texas
And were heading out of state
Down towards Mexico
And a date with fate

Their bikes were big and heavy
The riders tall and lean
Each one a master
At riding his machine

They heard chopper blades above them
The police were closing fast
They both looked up into the sky
They both looked up aghast

Muskratt hit a pothole
His bike began to slide
Caprillo hit him from behind
Putting a swift end to his ride

State troopers were on them now
Cars getting in their way
They looked at each other
As if suffice to say
We won't surrender will we
We will both die here today

THUNDERBIKE

The big bike, the Thunderbike
Is coming to town.

The other bikes who are his mates
Are gathering all around.

The combinations at their stations
Know what they have to do.

The despatch bikes in a row
Waiting for their cue.

The Police bikes out the back
Have left their radios on.

The big bike, the Thunderbike
Is coming into town.

CHILDREN OF A LESSER MOD

Their father's idyllic childhood
Was lost beyond recall.
They were children of a lesser Mod,
In an album of sepia photographs,
He tried to stand tall.
They were children of a lesser Mod,
In a British Home Stores Parka,
He didn't quite fit in.
He tried hard to get his hair just right,
With a self-conscious silly grin.
He wasn't really up to it,
This of course was true,
His sons were children of a lesser Mod.

BEAUTIFUL LOSER

He was unimaginative;
Moody;
Unfriendly sometimes;
Cocky;
Mean, certainly;
Bad, definitely.
And totally unreliable.

But when the chips were down,
He was always there for you.

He may have been a loser,
But he was a beautiful one.
He was my friend,
The beautiful loser.

RECORD CHASE GRAVEYARD

Pass your test on a tiny moped,
Then buy a big, big bike.
Why not go record chasing,
You can if you like.

Put a record on a café jukebox,
Get back before it ends.
You'll be a big bike hero,
It will impress your friends.

The record chase graveyard,
Chase the spinning disc.
The record chase graveyard,
Is it really worth the risk?

BIKERS FROM OUTER SPACE

We are worried in the village
And we must not lose face
We are being invaded now
By bikers from outer space

Their spaceship is parked in a field
Near old Rikers place
In its hold, 500 bikes
Close to that at any case

They don't appear in daylight
But at night they are everywhere
They haven't hurt anybody yet
But we wonder if they care

The riders wear flashy uniforms
Long trench coats touch the ground
The whole thing is really menacing
We know when they're around

We are worried in the village
And we must not lose face
Coz we are being invaded now
By bikers from outer space

RURAL RIDES

Terry Testa on his Vespa
Rides down a country lane
Hits a log and hurts his back
Lies howling by a drain

Joe the Rocker with his pram
Does press-ups in the rain
Coming down from Tuppy Town
He won't go there again

The under-cover scarecrow brother
Dick the Modernist
Makes a good impression
With his version of the Twist

Milky Lil, homogenised
Her breasts they stand
    apart
Bony Tony her Shetland
    pony
Pulls the doyly cart

Farmer Gren back again
From a European tour
Takes make-up from his
    case
Not losing his allure

Daisy Vamp in the Gypsy camp
Under the green wood tree
Waving 'Hi' to passers-by
And serving herbal tea

Holy Joe and his biker mates
All in this merry gang
Are teaching Danish tourists
The art of Cockney Slang

Terracotta Teddy Boys
Stay in the Pylon shield
Johnny Rubber in a bush
Dopey by the field

Skinhead Stan, a gentle man
Reads from a book of prose
Nettal Ned and his brother Fred
Scare a flock of crows

Terry Truck and his pet duck
Are swimming in the pond
Eating scraps of carrot cake
Of which both of them are fond

Savage sons all Bootie boys
Go pogo-sticking by
Blister sisters in a row
Waiting by a sty

Stanley Grimes reads The Times
As his court appearance looms
Betty Snow at the flower show
Cultivating blooms

Ron the Mod and his scooter mates
Riding unafraid
Do a Police pyramid
Whilst heading for the glade

Master Jock with his crook and smock
Is bound to have his say
Jonny Snetter on his old Lambretta
Is keen to get away

Dipthong Dick, the heretic
A friend of Bonneville Bob
Lifts his ghetto blaster
As he twiddles with the knob

Ton-up Ted, a big bike man
Is in his caravan asleep
When a head comes through the window
Calling him a creep

Haystack Gert is a big flirt
And the boys would all agree
She was on the pill and would be still
If she hadn't stopped for tea

Travis Snark, the village Nark
Tells coppers all he knows
Janet Blintz gives her hair a rinse
And wipes her runny nose

The Handy Dandy eating sugar candy
Leans his scooter against a stile
Modern Kate, his best mate
Loves him all the while

Rural Rides

BUT DO IT WITHOUT ME

OK you want a revolution this I can clearly see
OK start the revolution but do it without me
Bikes line up as far as the eye can see
Start the revolution but do it without me
At first the situation was frankly risible
But now these boys have guns that are clearly visible
Things are getting serious now you see
You'd better start the revolution
But do it without me
Without me OK

STICKING POINT

The Policeman looked at me and said,
'Six of your friends are dead,
You're gonna have to stick around,
Stick around, don't leave town.'

Six bikes went over the cliff
And you're on the edge looking down

You must stick around, stick around
Don't leave town

You must have been one of the party
But you're still on the ground

You must stick around, stick around
Don't leave town

'It seems strange to me,
That you're left alone here, you see.
I'm going to have to take your statement.
You're gonna have to stick around,
Stick around, don't leave town.'

Stick around, why don't you?
Don't leave town.

TRAGEDY ON THE RIVER

Dark night fast bike
Tragedy on the river
He had to get back home
His love he had to give her

He was riding too fast
He had to see her face again
He was riding too fast
In the driving rain

His bike hit the bridge
He went into the water
Never again would he see
His lovely wife and daughter

Dark night fast bike
Tragedy on the river
He had to get back home
His love he had to give her

MODS AND ROCKERS CONFLICT AT THE OLD PEOPLE'S HOME

Spotlights on their Zimmer frames
The Rockers have iron bars
The situation is quite dangerous
It could leave many scars

Police cars in the compound
Helicopters in the sky
How this really started
No one could answer why

Hippies and Teds get on their knees
And begin to pray
Things are getting serious
This will not go away

Mods and Rockers conflict at the old people's home
Can such things be?
Will this last much longer?
We shall have to wait and see

APOCALYPSE NOT NOW

Apocalypse? What now?
C'mon, not yet, Holy Cow.
OK, have it later if you must,
But not now eh? Not now.

Apocalypse OK if you must.
All that fire and blood and dust.
Apocalypse not yet eh? Not right now.
OK Apocalypse but not right now,
Not now Apocalypse, not now.

COVER-UP BY DEFINITION

They only wanted witnesses,
If they liked the things they said.
This was cover-up by definition.
The Jury men were encouraged
To look the other way.
This was a cover-up by definition.
The boy on the bike was dead,
Therefore, could not have his say,
Riding the road to perdition,
The accused had money,
that was plain to see.
This was a cover-up by definition.

MOTORCYCLE ROUNDUP

Motorcycle Michael was a man of wild extremes.
He wore a pinstripe jacket and tattered denim jeans.
On his head he wore a helmet of battered chrome
    design.
He was on his way to the Motorcycle Roundup.

The heartbreak brothers rode in style,
With chief stalking horse at their side.
They came around the mountain
With a sense of pride.
They were on their way to the Motorcycle Roundup.

The infant phenomenon came off the block
On a big bike twice her size.
To the tall toll man she said,
'There will be no compromise.'
She was on her way to the Motorcycle Roundup.

Glasses Gregson and his chums were bringing their
    guitars
'We shall play all night if they let us,' he said
To loud shouts of Hurrahs.
They were on their way to the Motorcycle Roundup.

The seven pillars of wisdom
Were standing on the grass.
Where idiot boy Bolimba was signing autographs.
He was on his way to the Motorcycle Roundup.

JOHNNY COLLECT

They didn't like him,
but they had to show respect.
He was a protection racketeer,
They called him Johnny Collect.

He was a snazzy dresser;
Hand-made suits, the works.
A top London Mod,
Not one of your scruffy jerks.

He made a good living,
Watching the punters squirm.
If they delayed a payment,
A beating they would earn.

They didn't like him,
but they had to show respect.
He was a protection racketeer,
They called him Johnny Collect.

BIG JACK BLACKOVRIAC

Big Jack Blackovriac
Was a motorcycle cop
Big Jack Blackovriac
Liked the job a lot

In his spare time though
He would often play
Tiddly winks in a bar
Down in old LA

RON DETTOL AND THE ONE-WAY TICKET TO PALOOKAVILLE

Ron Dettol loved his wife, and he loved his daughter.
Ron worked hard all day long as a Smithfield meat
porter.

On the weekends he would ride his scooter to the
coast
With his mates, all top Mods (the ones he liked the
most).

Ron Dettol was well hard; he was really tasty.
When he met Rockers though, he was very hasty.

He sometimes beat up two, or three of them at once.
Ron was quite intelligent; he was not a dunce.

When he was arrested for causing an affray,
It was headline news, embarrassing. It would not go
away.

Back home next day, his wife picked up the paper.
There was Ron, front page news – blimey what a
caper!

Ron's wife, her name was Blanche, said, 'It's come to
it,
I can't take this no longer.'

Ron looked at Blanche, he loved her so;
His love was growing stronger.

'I'm going out with Billy Smith, he is really classy,
He's not a bit like you, you're so bleedin' nasty.'

Ron realised the life he'd known was coming to an
    end,
And if he didn't watch himself, he could go round the
    bend.

The one-way ticket to Palookaville, he'd brought it
    on himself,
And if he wasn't careful, he would end up on the
    shelf.

Poor Ron.

ZEN AND THE ART

Correlated linear vision
Results in abject indecision
        Zen and the Art
Attitudinal sunset glances
Standing in for classic dances
        Zen and the Art
Sophomoric climate ranges
Are waiting now for cosmic changes
        Zen and the Art
Looking out in gliding fancies
Dissipates our dilettantes
        Zen and the Art
Spanners out and take it easy
Try not to make your fingers greasy
That tiny nut, that little beauty
Command it now to do its duty
        Zen and the Art
Wolf and dog are cousins now
Despite the dialectic row
        Zen and the Art

EAT DUST

You're in my rear-view mirror
As I'm pulling away.
Eat dust baby, eat dust.

The years I wasted following you
I know in my heart you could never be true.

You're drinkin' your coffee from an old cracked mug
You will never be the one to give me love.
Eat dust.
Eat my dust baby.
Eat dust!

DEATH BY COW

Up ahead he saw a steer
Don't look now death by cow
He saw the steer reappear
Don't look now death by cow
He changed the gear but it felt queer
He braked hard but it cost him dear
At once he heard the victim moo
But he was a victim too
Don't look now death by cow
Don't look now death by cow

GOTTA GO BOY, NO INSURANCE

I was driving my combination down a lane
When a truck came at me like a train
It was big and it was green
The biggest truck I've ever seen
I had to make a big decision
To try and avoid a big collision
But it was too late
Yes, it was too late
He crashed into my sidecar fender
And as far as I can remember
Knocked me in a ditch
Where my leg began to twitch
My sidecar it was smashed up badly
The handlebars were twisted sadly
And it was too late
Too late to escape this fate
'Are you alright son?' the driver said to me
'I've got to get away from here you see'
He gave a look of extreme abhorrence
He said 'I've got to go boy no insurance
Gotta go boy, no insurance'
To make it plain, I'll say it again
'Gotta go boy no insurance'
The truck it disappeared from view
I didn't know just what to do
I was left there all alone
It was before the days of mobile phone
What happened here I can't explain
His words kept going around my brain

'Gotta go boy no insurance'
'Gotta go boy no insurance'
'To make it plain I'll say it again'
'Gotta go boy no insurance'

THE VAMPIRE BIKERS OF BECKWITH TOR

The Vampire Bikers of Beckwith Tor
Were a screwy lot indeed.
Hell bent on their bloody quest,
They were filled with lust and greed.

They lay in wait
By the forest gate
For a passing caravan.

Then with whoops and screams
From some nightmare dreams,
They would slaughter every man.

The women they would take away
To join their atrocious group.
They would tie their hands with rubber bands.
They were really up the loop.

The Vampire Bikers of Beckwith Tor
Can't really be excused.
To all intents and purposes
They really were bad news.

They live in myth and legend now.
They were a rough old lot,
And a croaking toad by an old crossroad
Marks their favourite spot.

STURDY BEGGARS

Hark! Hark! The dogs do bark.
The bikers are coming to town.
Some in leather, some in rag,
Some in velvet gown.

Riding hard o'er rough terrain
Through desolate desert tracks.
Some come prepared to stay awhile
With blankets on their backs.

Living on a razor's edge
Their instincts finely honed.
To a man they can't remember
The last place they called home.

A lone wolf on a hunting spree
Picks up their rancid scent.
Baying now, a full moon howl.
He knows which way they went.

Hark! Hark! The dogs do bark.
The bikers are coming to town.
Some in leather, some in rag,
Some in velvet gown.

DIVORCED AND SLAUGHTERED

Divorced and slaughtered
The wife took everything he had
He wouldn't see his kids again
No-one to call him Dad

He sold his motorcycle
To try and makes things right
He is divorced and slaughtered

He lives on the streets now
Begging for his meals
You have to go through it
To know how it feels

You might walk past him
On your West End theatre night
He is divorced and slaughtered

TROUBLE IN TOMATO LAND

They grow tomatoes down here
They grow them really big
Two scooter chaps are caught up
In a Mods and Rockers gig
These chaps don't like punch ups
It's really not their scene
They wished they'd stayed playing cricket
On their village green
These tomatoes make great ammo
They've got a nasty splosh
Let's face it though dear reader
It's better than a cosh
These scooter chaps make haste
They'll get out if they can
Riding on their scooters
Behind a grocer's van
Trouble in tomato land
In this Mods and Rockers fight
It ends the next morning
But it went on all night

Green
Grocers

STEAMROLLER BLUES

Woke up this morning,
Pushed my motorcycle out the door.
Rode on up the road
Like I've done many times before.
I got those steamroller blues, baby.
Those pending steamroller blues.

Got to work on time,
Saw this steamroller in a bay.
I parked the bike in front of it
And went on my way.
I got those steamroller blues, baby.
Those pending steamroller blues.
I got those steamroller blues, baby.
Those blues is hard to lose.

Went down to get my rake
To start work raking tar.
I saw a big commotion
Thinking someone crashed a car.
I got those steamroller blues, baby.
Those pending steamroller blues.

I saw then what had happened
I'd never seen the like.
The man had started his roller up
And gone right over my bike.
I got those steamroller blues, baby.
Those serious steamroller blues.
I got those steamroller blues, baby.
Those blues is hard to lose.

I was nearly tearing my hair out
And yelling out with pain.
'Whose gonna pay out compensation?'
The driver said, 'Vic Thorneburrow is his name.'
I got those steamroller blues, baby.
Those hot tar steamroller blues.

I got a claim investigator
Who wanted twenty per
  cent.
I said, 'Fair enough,
  mister,
Just leave enough to pay
  my rent.'

I got those steamroller
  blues, baby.
Those claim investigator
  steamroller blues.
I got those steamroller
  blues, baby.
Those blues is hard to lose.

I got my dough from Vic Thorneburrow.
They let me keep what was left of the bike.
It was crushed beyond recognition
So I turned it into a trike.
I got those steamroller blues, baby.
Those Vic Thorneburrow steamroller blues.
I got those steamroller blues, baby.
Those blues is hard to lose.

RENEGADE NUNS ON WHEELS

Fed up with the vow of silence
Fed up with the dreary meals
Fed up with the life of solitude
Renegade nuns on wheels.

Gone is the vow of silence
It no longer now appeals
Mother Superior throws a fit
Renegade nuns on wheels.

Down into the valley
Onward to the hills
Four Harleys and an Indian
Renegade nuns
on wheels.

SCOOTER SKIN

Ricky Clifford; scooter skin.
Always out, never in.
There ain't nuffin he likes better
Than tinkerin' wiv his old Lambretta.

He's got it cut down, chopper style.
He rides upon it wiv a smile.
Out on runs wiv his mates.
He don't care how long it takes.

He likes his Reggae and the Ska.
He don't like riding in a car.
Goes out drinking wiv his best mate Barry.
They get pissed at every scooter rally.

He goes out riding on his tod.
(No, he's not an effin Mod.)
But he prefers it in a crowd.
Wiv the music really loud.

His weekends are most outrageous
And the mood is quite contagious.
People stomping to the beat.
He likes it that way; thinks it's sweet.

Up early Monday morning.
Goes to work. He's still yawning.
Soon the weekend comes around.
He'll be stomping to that Reggae sound.

PARANOID FRANCESCA

Paranoid Francesca had a fear of being alone.
She had this fear, when very young, of being on her
 own.
She was often isolated in her later life as well.
Why this should have happened, no-one could really tell.

She saw this man; handsome, strong; on a six fifty
 machine.
Leather clad in studs and stuff, his hair combed with
 a cream.
Her fluttered lids and make-up did not have the
 desired effect.
She tried in vain, once again, but sadly, she could not
 connect.

He would frequent the cafés and bars adjacent to her
 town.
With a gang, a motley crew, he would travel up and
 down.
To get him to take notice she bought herself a bike;
But jealous female suitors told her, 'Beat it, take a
 hike.'

Paranoid Francesca had a fear of being alone.
She had this fear, when very young, of being on her
 own.
She was often isolated in her later life as well.
Why this should have happened, no-one could really
 tell.

One night our hero and his mates were standing by the lake.

Someone spotted something floating. 'What's this, for heaven's sake?'

Our hero saw her lovely face, her sodden dark brown hair.

'She is lovely. She is dead. For God's sake, have a care.'

He lifted up her body and took it to the shore.
'Who is she? Where is she from? I've not seen her
  before.'
He was in love so deeply, but his love he could not
  save.
He followed in procession and stood weeping at her
  grave.
Paranoid Francesca had a fear of being alone.
She had this fear, when very young, of being on her
  own.
She was often isolated in her later life as well.
Why this should have happened, no-one could really
  tell.

ON ANY GIVEN......

On any given Monday
I'm with me mates down the pub.
On any given Tuesday
It's the same.
On any given Wednesday
I take me trail bike to the woods.
That's of course if it doesn't rain.
On any given Thursday
I go out for a ride
With me mates down the motorway.
On any given Friday
We all go down the coast.
On any given Saturday
That's where we stay.
On any given Sunday
We all ride back home.
I have a bath,
And then I feel O.K.

OH RAMONA!

Oh Ramona! Is it true?
Chicken Dave's in love with you?
Oh Ramona! It's not fair.
Buck teeth, glasses, stupid hair.
Does he really stand a chance?
He says he'll see you at the dance.

Oh Ramona! Is it true?
You're in love with Johnny Drew?
We don't blame you, he's so cool.
He's enough to make you drool.
Is this the start of true romance?
Will he take you to the dance?

Oh Ramona! Is it true?
Chicken Dave's upset with you?
He feels jilted, scorned, betrayed.
A victim of the trick you played.
Oh Ramona! Dangerous game.
Maybe you are not to blame.

Oh Ramona! You're so rare.
Lovely figure, sensuous stare.
Pristine beauty, wondrous face.
Classic bearing, Hellenic grace.
The boys all want you, this is true.
They are all aware of you.

Oh Ramona! Is it true?
Dave has challenged Johnny Drew.
He's acquired a powerful bike.
We have never seen the like.
Chicken Dave; and not for fun
Challenged Johnny Drew to a chicken run.

Oh Ramona! Stop it please.
We are begging on our knees.
They will ride the bikes, it's said
'Til one of them ends up dead.
Across the main road riding blind.
Please Ramona, please be kind.

Oh Ramona! We're in black.
Dave and Johnny won't come back.
Dying on their chicken run.
Done for honour, not for fun.
But in our hearts, we are   so blue.
Both died for the love   of you.

NOT VERY PLEASED MAX

Not Very Pleased Max
Would review his situation,
Finding he was nowhere near
Apocalypse annihilation.

He would have to go in training, though,
Knowing time wasn't on his side.
Eating dog food from a can
Was not beneath his pride.

Soft civilization had indeed
Seemed to make him weak.
He would have to toughen up, you see,
To get it together, so to speak.

He went on a fitness bender,
Running; jogging every night.
Shadow boxing down the lane,
He would have to get it right.

Not Very Pleased Max
Was steeped in absolute corruption.
But missed the post-nuclear void
Of violence and destruction.

Not Very Pleased Max
Was an irritable bastard.
His girlfriend's name was Jenny Smith
And it was good while it lasted.

He was fond of Mel Gibson
But didn't really have his looks,
And was seriously impressed
By those motorcycle crooks.

Not Very Pleased Max
Was bored with nine to five,
And to show what he could do
He needed total strife.

Not Very Pleased Max
Is rugged, tough and bad.
So, whatever you do, mates
Don't ever make him mad.

NORM'S GOLD WING

Bumped into Norm six months ago.
'Hello, mate. How's your Gold Wing?'
He said, 'Well, I've got a problem.
I've gone and hurt the thing.'

I asked Norm to explain.
Eventually he did.
He put it in for a service,
To this cocky fresh-faced kid.

Farmers was the name of the firm,
And I'd heard of them alright.
Norm said they'd phoned him up,
And what they said gave him a fright.

'Your engine's got a hole in it.'
The bloke was quite polite.
'That's strange.' thought Norm,
'I could have sworn everything was alright.'

'Are they responsible for it, Norm?'
'Well they said that they are not.
And the bloke said to put it right
Was going to cost a lot.'

Well, days and weeks and months went past.
Norm said that he'd lost track.
So I thought that I would help him out
And try to get it back.

So I rode down to Farmers
On my old Honda Four.
'Yes, sir. Can we help you?'
Said the bloke behind the door.

'I want to have a service.'
'Ah. You've come to the right place.'
The bloke had hollow looking eyes.
There was a smirk upon his face.

'Can I see your workshop?'
'Yes, of course. It's through the gate.'
And there was Norm's combo,
And it was in a right old state.

There was tea stains on the leather seat,
Coffee cup marks on the chair,
Take away trays on his top box,
I had to get away from there.

Farmers closed soon after that
And Norm got his Gold Wing back.
Still in the same condition, mind.
I gave Norm some serious flak.

We could see now what had happened.
With a notebook we took stock.
When trying to remove the rad
The kid had drilled right through the block.

Norm rang me sometime later.
He was full of the joys of spring.
'I've got me a mechanic
To help me with me Wing.'

I asked, 'Where did he hail from?
You know, which neck of the wood?'
Norm said, 'He used to work for Farmers
So he must be pretty good!'

True story

MURDER MILE

Take a trip down murder mile.
Put a shilling in the jukebox. Do it in style.

Get to the roundabout and back again.
Do it before the record ends.

You can do it to your favourite song.
But remember you must not take too long.

You could get killed, but it's all in the game.
Poor lorry driver won't be to blame.

Murder mile - Murder Mile.
Do it café racer style.
Your girl will be waiting there
Back at the caff combing her hair.

You could be a hero here tonight.
Let's hope you can get it right.

MURDER BALL MOD

He played Murder Ball at school
He was the Murder Ball Mod
He didn't play football or cricket at all
He was the Murder Ball Mod

He played Murder Ball
        Murder Ball
        Murder Ball

He was the Murder Ball Mod

When he left school, he got a job in Fleet Street
He was the Murder Ball Mod
He dressed cute in his mohair suit
He was the Murder Ball Mod

He still played Murder Ball
    Still played Murder Ball

He was the Murder Ball Mod

MOD'S REUNION

It was a day of celebration
In local history.
The old Mods got their scooters out
Circa '63.

'Mohair' Freddy Johnson
Still had his one seven five,
And Terry Smith his old Sportique,
More dead than alive.

Lil 'The Pill' from Leesons Hill
Was on the back of Sammy Pierce.
Reggie Stone still on his own
After thirty years.

Johnny 'Pinstripe' Collier
With his chromed T.V.
And 'Fab Tab' Micky Sarsons
Arrived on his G.T.

Eric 'The Swede' Larson
Still had the same French crop
But 'Shorty' Sammy Matthews
Was losing his on top.

'Bluebeat' Vic Dennison
With the same old pork pie hat;
We told him that it suited him
But we thought he looked a prat.

'Braces' Johnny Jones turned up
With his best mate Jimmy Green,
And his cousin 'Crewneck' Wilson
Who looked like Steve McQueen.

The fabulous 'Pinkie' came at last
(also known as the Brighton Rock).
His girl was wearing glass heeled shoes
With 'I really love him' on her frock.

One of the late arrivals
Was 'The Quiet Man' Roger Smith,
On his black GS one sixty,
With his hair in Sixties quiff.

We danced to Sixties music.
It really was a thrill.
Ricky Philips sorted it
But we helped him with the bill.

We did The Dog and The Watusi,
The Shake, The Twist, The Slide.
Some of the boys got fed up
And took their scooters for a ride.

We were sorry it was over.
We all had a good laugh.
And we all stood together
For a nostalgia photograph.

Not all the boys could make it.
Some of them were dead.
We had a minute's silence
And a little prayer was said.

MISS WELD

She was a real cutie
A stunning beauty queen
She wore a low-cut top
In the welding shop
When fixing those machines

She was a great mechanic
She knew how to mend a bike
She'd strip an engine down
Without a frown
She knew how to do it right

When she went out in the evenings
She rode an old BSA
She looked real sweet
Riding down the street
She'd take your breath away

Miss Weld

MARGINALIZED MILTON

Marginalized Milton was fed up with his life.
He'd lost his job and fallen out with his wife.
She'd just moved in with his best mate Tel,
Taking the kids Dean and Michelle.
Milt dragged his Lambretta up to the top of his flat.
When he rode off the side Milt thought, 'That will be
    that.'

He made him a ramp out of timber and rope.
At the chance of a new life, Milt had given up hope.
A crowd had gathered, coming in from the park.
Milt shouted, 'Stand back, folks,' as it was getting
    near dark.
He spoke to the crowd through a stolen loud hailer
That he'd recently nicked from a cub scout Arkala.

Milt put on his Doc Martens for the last time,
Feeling his life had run out of reason and rhyme.
He always felt as safe as houses
When he was wearing his camouflage trousers.
Only now Milton felt he had nowhere to go
And he didn't care for being treated like a shmo.

He was being pursued by the CSA
And the CAB had no more to say.
The woman down at the DHS
Looked a lot like Rudolph Hess.
Marginalized Milton wrote his mum a note.
He felt a small lump well up in his throat.

Marginalized Milton was not a success.
He now found his life was really a mess.
He felt his day was a hopeless drag
As he stood there and lit his twenty-fifth fag.
Marginalized Milton had but a short time to live
Which was a shame coz Milt had so much to give.

He launched his Lambretta out into the night.
At last, Milt thought, he'd got something right.
The crowd were filled with kindness and love.
The Lambretta light shone like the moon up above.
Milt looked like he belonged to the stars
Before he crashed down to the line of parked cars.

The summoned dead divas of reggae and soul
Came to take him away to his ultimate goal.
The people were crying, nothing was said.
They knew in their hearts; poor Milton was dead.
The proud Lambretta seemed broken and bent.
Perhaps it too was now heaven sent.

Marginalized Milton, your life wasn't a crime.
You were but a player in this space and time.
Dean and Michelle were at their dad's grave.
Tel and Milt's wife said they were quite brave.
Given the breaks, Milt, it could have been better
But at least you were given a trusty Lambretta.

LONG GONE JACK

My baby she was heavy, heavy
With my child.
I just looked at her,
Looked at her and smiled.

I'm long gone Jack,
Don't intend to stick around.
I'll get my motorcycle revvin',
Start heading outa town.

I know I'm no good,
A bum, don't you see?
An' can't seem to bother with
My responsibility.

I'm long gone Jack, don't intend
To stick around.
Get my motorcycle revvin'
Start heading outa town.

LOATHSOME COWBOY

He'll be riding down the mountain when he comes.
Yippee I kiyay
He's riding into town again.
Here comes the loathsome cowboy.

He would have had a horse, of course.
But that was out of time for him.
Technology has given him a powerful machine.
It would seem that men like him don't change.
They never tow the line.
He never loves but commits some sort of emotional
crime;
every time.

Some say he has a heart.
As yet no-one has been able to prove it.
Yippee I kiyay.
Get away... fast.
Here comes the loathsome cowboy.

JOHNNY THE MOD

He was hanging in a tree when they
    found him.
Hanging dead in a tree.
His scooter lay smashed
Where he'd crashed
But he was hanging in a tree.
Hanging by his braces in a tree.
Johnny the Mod had gone to God
In the summer of '63.

JOHN WAYNE SKIES

My girl said, 'Never leave me'
And tears filled her eyes.
I told her that I loved her
But it was mostly lies.

I'm proud to be an Englishman.
One you won't despise.
But I looked across her shoulder
At those John Wayne skies.

I live in this small island
But it's big in my eyes.
It's John Ford country
With John Wayne skies.

When I'm on the motorway
Metal tank between my thighs.
I'm a fearless desperado
Who will never compromise.

I won't be condescending
And I never patronise
But I'm in John Ford country
With John Wayne skies.

I know I'm getting older
And the time it really flies.
I'd better ride into the sunset
To those John Wayne skies.

A fearless desperado
Who will never compromise
In John Ford country
With John Wayne skies.

To the left of centre
Just above the rise
Comes a band of hostile redskins
With hatred in their eyes.

I move the bike a little forward
From their whoops and cries.
As they stream down the mountain
From those John Wayne skies.

GLADIATOR (THE YOB)

A yob at over fifty, lads.
I'm going on fifty-four.
Spartacus Bikus Maximus.
Rotten to the core.

Dangerous boys and tearaways,
I won't take it anymore.
From Brand's Hatch to Elvingdon,
I've seen it all before.

I've done my share of racing.
I was a demon on the track.
I rode the tar,
Smelt the "Castrol R",
But I can't find my way back.

The good girls used to shun us
When we started years ago.
I was Spartacus Bikus Maximus
Just putting on a show.

JILTED AT THE ALTAR

Some of the boys rode down to the West Country in the summer of nineteen sixty-five. On arrival at a small fishing village, they decided to have a beer at one of the local pubs.

Mick stood outside watching this old lady collecting car numbers; she was writing on one of those shiny toilet rolls which were popular at the time. She had gathered lots of numbers and the toilet paper was dragging on the ground.

When Mick enquired inside the pub as to who the old lady was and why she was doing this, the woman behind the bar said, 'Oh, that's old Meg, she was jilted at the altar in nineteen twenty-six and she saw her intended husband in a car looking back at her as the car drove away and she's been collecting numbers ever since. There weren't many cars around in 1926, not like now eh? Sad though, isn't it?'.

All the boys agreed.

True story.

FEAR AND LOATHING ON THE KING'S HIGHWAY

Four riders ride out
Hell bent on disarray
Four killer riders
On the King's Highway

Big bike riders
Quick to join the fray
Hell bent for leather
On the King's Highway

A fat cat driver
Comes the other way
He begs for mercy
On the King's Highway

They take his money
And kill him anyway
The big bike riders
On the King's Highway

A poor van driver
Seems to lose his way
He asks directions
On the King's Highway

They burn his van
But they let him get away.
The four killer riders
On the King's Highway

Fear and loathing on the King's Highway
Fear and loathing on the King's Highway
Three brothers and a cousin on the King's Highway
Big bike riders hell bent on disarray
Bad seed riders on the King's Highway.

A troupe of players come their way
'Come and join us friends,' they say.
But they kill them anyway.
Leave them dead on the King's Highway.
Dead and dying on the King's Highway.
Bad seed killers have their way.
Fear and loathing on the King's Highway.

A wayside trader knows the score
When they hang him by the door
And nail his wife to the old oak floor.
They take their leave with a deafening roar.
Big bike riders have their way
Bad seed killers on the King's Highway
What will they do on judgement day?
Fear and loathing on the King's Highway

GIRL ON A MOTORCYCLE

Girl on a motorcycle
Do as you like;
Black leather terminator;
Supersonic stator plater;
Hi-tech minge eliminator;
Carburetor jetter setter;
Super wimp immobilizer;
Tensile techno tarmac glider;
She-wolf leggy saddle strider;
Sexy wrist accelerator;
Super speed administrator;
Super highway dominator.
Girl on a motorcycle
Do as you like.

DOCTOR ROCKER AND MISTER MOD

The two-headed apparition is indeed a
  schizophrenic.
This argument may reach the dizzy heights of the
  polemic
Which leaves us with an answer which is purely
  academic.
Doctor Rocker and Mister Mod.

Existing functions which continue to elude the social
strata
Headlines brimming over with exaggerated data.
The zooter suiter, hostile scooter, punitive reactor.
Doctor Rocker and Mister Mod.

The overwhelming ad hoc, yob rock, old hard-core
collective
Did indeed go to speed, the new dance hall directive
Making the whole procession a darn sight more
effective.
Doctor Rocker and Mister Mod.

Lacking now the laden bough of corporative
delusion.
Rolling on in merry song of deliberate illusion,
With base feeling, reeling now with tabloid terse
intrusion.
Doctor Rocker and Mister Mod.

DEATH RIDES A BIKE

Death rides a bike,
Came careering down the road.
Showing off to all his mates,
The stupid little toad.
Didn't see the old girl
Pull out from her drive.
Now he's dead as a dodo,
But she's still alive.

THE ROCKER'S MOTHER

They had a picture on the wall
Of a white-haired lady in a shawl

She was the Rocker's mother
      The Rocker's mother
      The Rocker's mother

The picture was really kinda sad
She had seven sons that all went bad

She was the Rocker's mother
      The Rocker's mother
      The Rocker's mother

Four banged up Lewes way
Three lived in Kent in old North Cray

> The Rocker's mother
> The Rocker's mother
> The Rocker's mother

So, think before you commit a crime
You won't be the only one doing time
Spare a thought for the Rocker's mother.

The Rocker's mother

BIG BIKE BORE

I met him at a bike meet.
I'd seen him there before.
He went on about Brit bikes.
He was a Big Bike Bore.

Now I like British bikes.
They rank among the best.
But I'm averse to prejudice.
I'll get that off me chest.

"My first bike was a C15,
I've had British bikes for years.
My next bike was an A.J.S."
He was boring me to tears.

"Then I had a Gold Star,
Then a big Gold Flash.
Better than this foreign muck.
That stuff's all just trash."

"Then I bought a Thunderbird,
Then a pre-unit Bonnie,
Then an Aerial Square Four combo,
From me Uncle Johnny."

"A Royal Enfield Super Meteor,
Then a Constellation,
Then a smashing Interceptor,
From a porter at the station."

94

"Then I bought a Leader,
Then a J.A.P.
That wasn't a foreign bike.
You can take it from me."

It was all too much for me.
I couldn't take much more.
When I walked up to my Gold Wing,
His jaw dropped to the floor.

When it comes to conversation,
He is really the last straw.
He goes on and on and on.
He's just a Big Bike Bore.

BORN AGAIN BRIAN

Born again Brian
A pretender to the throne
Didn't like his life pre-bike
Spending too much time alone.

He'd passed his test years ago
In August nineteen sixty-three.
He passed first time, he felt sublime,
On his little 'Fanny B'.

But for over thirty years
Brian hadn't had a bike.
Some of these modern ones were great.
He'd never seen the like.

He bought a big Seven Fifty
But his reactions now were slow.
His new mates tried to egg him on
But he just had to let them go.

He had a chat with his wife
Who said, 'Bri, trade it in.'
She pointed to a 'Twist and Go'
Which she thought would quite suit him.

So in the end Brian agreed
And now he goes out with his wife.
They go touring every weekend.
It's really changed his life.

So the moral to this little tale
Is to do what's right for you
And to know your limitations
And to your own self be true.

THE BROTHERS DUTCH

As the brothers Dutch were riding
They saw an eagle in the sky
Sky west and crooked
Very high it did fly.

Sky west and crooked,
Out towards the sea
As the brothers Dutch were riding
To meet their destiny.

They rode to meet the old noon train
Their killer already there.
He surprised the brothers Dutch
Shot them down without a care.

As the brothers Dutch were riding
They saw an eagle in the sky
Sky west and crooked
Very high it did fly.

THE BALLAD OF JED LAW AND VALENTINE

Said Jed Law to Valentine,
'The girl that you're with all the time
I would like to make her mine
And for her I'd take the time
To race you out along the line
From Johnsons' to the Dutch House sign
And do it all in quicker time
And do it just to make her mine,'
Said Jed Law to Valentine.

And Valentine he took the bait
And because Jed was his mate
He had a drink to celebrate
And let the gods decide their fate.
To race his friend, it was decreed
That the one with greater need
Would be the one with greater speed,
To race his friend and ride the line
From Johnsons' to the Dutch House sign.

Said Bobby Lee to Valentine,
'The friend that you're with all the time
Would race you to the Dutch House sign
And if he wins, I understand
He'd be the one to win my hand.
Do I get a say in this?
Do I choose the one to kiss?
The one to love for all time.
How I love you, Valentine.'

Valentine he smiled and said,
'I know that you are fond of Jed
And he knows that you are mine.
Because of this we ride the line
From Johnsons' to the Dutch House sign
And do it all in quicker time
For love of you', said Valentine.

At two a.m. on Solstice Day
The race it was soon underway.
Marshalls saw there was fair play
All the way along the line
From Johnsons' to the Dutch House sign.
Triumph versus B.S.A.
At two a.m. on Solstice day.
All the way along the line
From Johnsons' to the Dutch House sign
'For love of you,' said Valentine.

Machines produced a thunder roar
And both riders knew the score.
Racing now along the line
From Johnsons' to the Dutch House sign.
Now one rider was ahead;
First Valentine then Jed.
Pretty soon they'd both be dead.
Riding down along the line
From Johnsons' to the Dutch House sign.

Valentine he had to swerve
As poor Jed he hit the curve.
They died about the same time
Did Jed Law and Valentine.
Somewhere there along the line
From Johnsons' to the Dutch House sign.
And the one with greater speed
Shall be the one with greater need.
To do it all in quicker time.
'For love of you,' said Valentine.

Bobby Lee, she didn't wed.
She nursed a broken heart they said.
Never to forget her Jed
And her darling Valentine
Who would gladly ride the line
From Johnsons' to the Dutch House sign
And do it all in quicker time
'For love of you,' said Valentine.

If you venture out at Solstice time
Somewhere there along the line
From Johnsons' to the Dutch House sign
Two ghostly riders can be seen
Each one on his own machine
Riding now as in a dream
Riding now along the line
From Johnsons' to the Dutch House sign
And to do it all in quicker time
'For love of you,' said Valentine.

HOW DID WE DO?

I'm down here at the speedway track,
Had a job at the Mill but they gave me the sack.

How did we do boy? How did we do boy?
     How did we do?

I'll get me a team; I'll do what it takes.
Just remember these bikes don't have no brakes.

How did we do boy? How did we do boy?
     How did we do?

I got Limey Pete, and Billy McGraw.
The faster we go, these boys want more.

How did we do boy? How did we do boy?
     How did we do?

We're gonna win, I feel it in my water.
I got me a date, with the Manager's daughter.

How did we do boy? How did we do boy?
     How did we do?

          Tell us how we did!

OIK

That blighter on that motorbike
I have never seen the like
Oik Oik, Oik Oik Oik
He has no mater; has no pater
And he has no Alma Mater
Oik Oik, Oik Oik Oik
No, he's not an Oxbridge blue
Not like me, not like you
Oik Oik, Oik Oik Oik
Not at Eton, not at Harrow
His forehead is far too narrow
Oik Oik, Oik Oik Oik
Can't play cricket, can't play rugger
Bet he is a useless bugger
Oik Oik, Oik Oik Oik
No profession waits for him
His fortune then is pretty grim
Oik Oik, Oik Oik Oik
Won't go rowing with the squad
Is he a Rocker or a Mod?
Oik Oik, Oik Oik Oik
In wartime he won't make the grade
In a trench with a spade
Oik Oik, Oik Oik Oik
A gardener or a labourer he
Cannon fodder, don't you see?
Oik

TAKE ME TO YOUR LEADER

Take me to your leader
I know he is the one
He rides a Vespa scooter
He disappears into the sun

He is like a shepherd
Caring for his flock
He will be taken seriously
Please don't stand and mock

We will follow anywhere
Follow him to the end
We will follow down the Highway
Follow round the bend

He is the leader
Although we ride three abreast
He is the leader
The one we like the best

ROCKERS REVOLT

Rockers are revolting in our village
Like the peasants in 1381
Rockers are revolting in our village
Revolting every mother's son

They are not upset about their wages
And they are not doing it for fun
Rockers are revolting in our village
Revolting every mother's son

They are aggrieved by Mods and Beatniks
It seems they are everywhere
The nature of the cafés and bars is changing
And the Rockers don't think it's fair

Rockers are revolting in our village
Like the peasants in 1381
Rockers are revolting in our village
Revolting every mother's son

Rockers Revolt

NEVER LOOK AWAY

I met this old geezer on a BSA
He said: Never look away boy
Never look away

Some people say that they're your friend
Be with you until the end
But be that as it may
Never look away boy
Never look away

Don't you be nobody's fool
Keep your eye upon the ball
Be nice, be friendly, that's okay
But be careful what you say

Over the hills and far away
Never look away boy
Never look away

Well that is my philosophy
Here is half a crown, have a drink on me

He kicked his bike and I heard him say,
Never look away boy, never look away

Never look away boy
Never look away

MOTORCYCLE LEGEND

He was a legend
Never to be forgotten
He was a legend
Never to be forgotten

Didn't care who he trod on
To get to the bottom
Ruthless in reverse
Crazy, don't you see?
He really was his own worst enemy

Apparently

Isn't he a bit like you and me?

MANHUNT

He's out there on the Highway
And he's got a gun
A bad seed killer
A friend to no-one

MANHUNT

He's a big bike rider
A desperado you might say
A natural born killer
Keen to get away

MANHUNT

He robbed a gas station
Down in San Antone
Robbed a gas station
Did it on his own

MANHUNT

Robbed a gas station
Shot the teller dead
Then he murdered a family
There's a big price on his head

MANHUNT

KICKSTART

He'd hit his girlfriend with a brick
He was feelin' kinda sick
Was she dead? He didn't know
He didn't mean to do it.

His bike was standing on its stick
He gave the machine a mighty kick
Was she dead? He didn't know
He didn't mean to do it.

He rode for miles on the old Highway
He had ridden far that day
But the thought wouldn't go away
I didn't mean to do it.

He went into a Roadhouse Bar
A plain-clothes watched him from his car
'Yes, he fit the photofit'
But did he mean to do it?

He went for a gun in his coat
The plain-clothes shot him in the throat
In his hand, he found a note
'I didn't mean to do it'

'I didn't mean to do it'
'I didn't mean to do it'
In his hand, he found a note
'I didn't mean to do it'

JOHN CARUTHERS DE LA MERE

John Caruthers de la Mere
Rode his bike without a care
Riding round his vast estate
Through the valley to the gate

He wouldn't wear a helmet though
He thought it was the way to go
Wouldn't wear a helmet, but
When he hit the gaping rut
He swerved to miss a spotted toad
Sitting there upon the road
He broke his neck at once you see
The bike, it crashed into a tree

John Caruthers de la Mere
Rode his bike without a care
Riding round his vast estate
Through the valley to the gate

IMITATION MOD

He wore all the right gear
But it was because
He was the imitation Mod

He bought a cool Lambretta
A Pacemaker 150
It was a smashing scooter
Really fast and nifty

But in his heart of hearts
He was a Rocker through and through
He yearned for a Triumph Bonneville
Between me and you

He wore all the right gear
But it was because
He was the imitation Mod

He sold the Lambretta
To his best mate Ronnie
Bought a brand new Thunderbird
(A cousin to the Bonnie)

He wore all the right gear
But it was because
He was the imitation Mod

He was happy now
To thine own self be true
Because in his heart of hearts
He was a Rocker through and through

The Imitation Mod

BE MY BABY

Be my baby
Be my baby
Be my baby
On a Saturday night

We'll go to the café
on the green
Put some money
in the record machine

Be my baby
Be my baby
Be my baby
On a Saturday night

I put my faith
in the Bonneville Boys
Dressed in leather
they make lots of noise

Be my baby
Be my baby
Be my baby
On a Saturday night

They are all good-natured
that's a fact
If they take you out
they will bring you back

Be my baby
Be my baby
Be my baby
On a Saturday night

BRAINS OF A ROCKING HORSE

She was blonde, she was coarse,
She had the brains of a rocking horse.
I asked her if we could go steady,
She said, 'Dunno mate, don't fink I'm ready.'

We rode down to The Rising Sun,
She had a bike but we used my one.
I introduced her to my mate Len,
He took her up the road and back again.

He said, 'I like your bird, she's real good-looking',
She said, 'I like you Len, 'ere, what's cookin?'
I left her for a bird called Heather,
I think her and Len are still together.

For a little while anyway,
Know what I mean?

ACE-FACE TWENTY-SIX

When light strikes me a certain way
I'm almost handsome, wouldn't you say?
But be this as it may
I'm Ace-Face Twenty-Six

There are a lot more crowd-pleasers
A lot of other tasty geezers
A lot of boys from different areas
Makes my position a bit precarious

We come together down the coast
We are the ones they dig the most
All of us from different places
Lots of other Mod-type faces

We are now south of the border
And to fit me in this pecking order
Just to fit me in the mix
I'LL BE ACE-FACE TWENTY-SIX

THE ROCKER AND THE BEAT

I know that you're a-grieving
Said the Rocker to the Beat
I know you loved your mother
(he tried to be discreet)
I know you feel alone now
Because she was all you had
But life goes on you know
Even though it's all so sad
Death surrounds us always
We know that this is true
But you must take heart my friend
Coz life surrounds us too
We all lose our loved ones
But we must be gentle in our grief
There's not one house that's known no suffering
That is my belief
He parked his motorcycle
He was off to buy a loaf of bread
The Beat felt strengthened now
By the words the Rocker said
We all lose our loved ones
But we must be gentle in our grief
There is not one house that has known no suffering
That is my belief

THE EDUCATED MOD

He was an educated Mod he
Not Secondary Modern like you and me
He was in the Chelsea scene
He didn't come from Bethnal Green
When he said 'Mate' he used the 't'
He didn't round it off like you and me
He wore sheepskin coats and jackets
His mohair must have cost a packet
His girls were more like debutantes
He was an educated Mod, see?
His scooter was the best by far
Sometimes he drove a Jaguar
Top down as he rode through town
He was an educated Mod, see?
He didn't work in Billingsgate
He didn't live on the estate
He was something in the city he
Not dockers sons like you and me
He was an iconoclast
He was going places fast
He was from a different class
His shoes were made from a last
He was an educated Mod
He was an educated Mod, see?
He was an educated Mod he
An educated Mod

THE INCREDIBLE SHRINKING MOD

He said a witch gave him a
   shrinking potion
And now he is charged with high
   emotion
He is the Incredible Shrinking Mod

His scooter was a real nice fit
Now he is too small for it

His clothes no longer wearable
Now life is unbearable
He is the Incredible Shrinking Mod

His girlfriend said she likes his tan
But now she needs a bigger man
Getting smaller every day
This malaise is here to stay

Life is hard for the Incredible Shrinking Mod

THE THEATRE GIRLS CLUB

The Theatre Girls Club
Was a place in Soho Square
I worked around the corner
I used to park my motorcycle there
It was a place for showgirls
That had got too old
Some of them resided there
Others sheltered
From the cold
One day I saw an elderly resident
Standing by a tree
Singing, 'Out of the darkest night he comes to me'
'Out of the darkest night he comes to me'
That was thirty years ago
And those words are with me still
That old lady's memory never left me
And perhaps it never will

Out of the darkest night he comes to me
The Theatre Girls Club

True story

WE ARE THE MIDS

This ain't about Mods
This ain't about Rockers
We are the Mids
Mids not Mockers

We wear black Beatle jackets
High heeled Beatle boots
White shirts, collar and tie
And we don't ride bikes or scoots

This ain't about Mods
This ain't about Rockers
We are the Mids
Mids not Mockers

In the sea-side riots
We will stand aloof
We're the inbetweenies
Mids, the living proof

This ain't about Mods
This ain't about Rockers
We are the Mids
Mids not Mockers

We are the Mids

LONELY JANET

Janet was a fifties queen
On those hot rock summer nights.
Seen around the caffs and bars
In sequined lurex tights.

She was a motorcycle diva
On her bitchin' pillion seat.
A leather scene sex siren
She would soon attract the heat.

The boys would snap their fingers
To the Cadent jukebox song,
And Janet stood like granite
Amidst the leather throng.

But that was forty years ago
And time has took its toll
On a motorcycle diva,
Queen of rock 'n roll.

She walks with fallen arches now
In a shuffled bending gait.
She lives in a block of flats
In a vast brick walled estate.

She often thinks about the time
When she was queen of the pack,
But she knows in her heart of hearts
There is no turning back.

And that was forty years ago
And time has took its toll
On poor lonely Janet
Queen of rock 'n roll.

AMY SURPLUS CARRADIN

Amy Surplus Carradin
Bought Army surplus on a whim.

In her shed behind the houses
Are piles of ex-Army trousers.

Navy coats, some double-breasted
Her savings were thus invested.

Air Force caps, assorted skirts
Parkas, boots and combat shirts.

Fatigue jackets, camouflage
In sizes small to extra-large.

Amy Surplus Carradin
Bought Army surplus on a whim.

LONG JOHN DELL

Gather round, folks, and kindly listen
To the tale I have to tell.
About the scooter boy and Pirates,
The daring Long John Dell.

It were a stormy night in the Harbour town
And the locals knew full well,
That the spok, spok, spok
On the flagstone path
Was the sound of Long John Dell.

Motley crew sat about the Inn.
'Ahoy to you, mate,' they cried.
'Avast, mates, it's rum for me,'
And to the wench behind the bar,
'You'd make a pretty bride.'

'It's rough out, mates,' said Long John Dell.
'In fact, I've never seen it worse.
'cepting once mebbe, goin' round the 'orn.'
A man stood up with full black beard,
A buccaneer for sure.
'You're too quiet about adventures, mate,
Come on, Long John, tell us more.'

But before Long John could say a word,
The door flew open wide.
A young boy maybe twelve or so
Stood shivering there inside.

'A ship is stranded on the rocks,
Them folks will die for sure!'
'Help is at hand,' said Long John Dell,
'Gimme ten strong men, no more.'

They launched a boat, a sturdy craft,
Mods and Rockers either side.
Ten men to the rowing, thus
Eleven men did glide,
Rising up the mountain crest,
Crashing down the other side.

They came upon the stricken ship,
Up to the stricken crew,
With grappling iron and cable
Forcibly Long John threw.

They saw the hook take hold,
The ship would now be saved.
Three cheers for Long John Dell,
Never was a man so brave.
But unbeknownst to anyone,
The rope had coiled 'round Long John's Leg.
Not his good one you understand,
His other one, the peg.
And with a crack he disappeared,
Impossible to save.
To Davy Jones' locker, boys,
And to a watery grave.

Ten years have passed,
Nay, twenty more.
Listen! What's that sound?
That spok, spok, spoking,
On the flagstone ground
It's a grizzly spectre, mate,
And anyone 'ere can tell.
It's the shimmering gait
Of your Pirate scooter boy, mate,
The daring Long John Dell.

THE BUTCHER'S ROCKER AND THE BAKEHOUSE MOD

The Rocker worked in a butcher's shop
At the far end of the town.
The Mod worked in the Bakehouse.
There was no common ground.

Butcher's Rocker,
Bakehouse Mod,
Butcher's Rocker,
Bakehouse Mod.

One weekend down the coast;
Not far from the station,
The Butcher's Rocker saw the Mod,
And he wanted aggravation.

Butcher's Rocker,
Bakehouse Mod,
Butcher's Rocker,
Bakehouse Mod.

The Butcher's Rocker and his mates
Chased the Bakehouse Mod.
The Bakehouse Mod was all alone,
Well and truly on his tod.

Butcher's Rocker,
Bakehouse Mod,
Butcher's Rocker,
Bakehouse Mod.

The Bakehouse Mod ran on the beach,
Into the foaming Brine.
To all intents and purposes,
The end of the line.

Butcher's Rocker,
Bakehouse Mod,
Butcher's Rocker,
Bakehouse Mod.

The Mod was drifting out to sea,
He wasn't a good swimmer.
Things could not be worse for him,
Nothing could be grimmer.

Butcher's Rocker,
Bakehouse Mod,
Butcher's Rocker,
Bakehouse Mod.

The Butcher's Rocker acted swift,
Took off his leather jacket.
It was real good quality,
Cost him quite a packet.

Butcher's Rocker,
Bakehouse Mod,
Butcher's Rocker,
Bakehouse Mod.

He dived into the crashing foam,
The temperature near zero.
He saved the life of the Bakehouse Mod,
He became a local hero.

Butcher's Rocker,
Bakehouse Mod,
Butcher's Rocker,
Bakehouse Mod.

Years later, now old friends,
They often reminisce,
About the swinging sixties
And the life of youthful bliss.

Butcher's Rocker,
Bakehouse Mod,
Butcher's Rocker,
Bakehouse Mod.

TOO TOUGH TO DANCE

From the wrong side of the tracks
He came looking for romance.
Went to the dance hall
Thought he'd take a chance.
But he just had to face it;
He was too tough to dance.

Motorcycle hero, size eleven shoe.
Jeans and leather jacket
Just like the rest of his crew.
He watched the buck and jive.
They knew just what to do.

The girls flocked around him.
They began to wonder why.
He looked at them with a twinkle in his eye.
Suddenly they realised,
He was too tough to dance.

He loved Donald O'Connor
And idolised Gene Kelly.
He liked Fred Astaire.
He'd seen him on his uncle's telly.
But the boy couldn't help it,
He was just too tough to dance.

Eventually he met a girl and settled down.
They lived with his mother
On the other side of town.
And he's still on his motorcycle
Riding up and down.

So, it seems he found his true romance.
He's got three kids. Jackie, Sue and Lance.
And the boy's like his daddy,
He just too tough to dance.

WILD TO BE BORN

I didn't ask to be here, man.
It wasn't up to me.
I'm angry about it.
Angry, that's me.

My parents were good.
Always good to me.
I didn't want to let them down.
Can't help it, can't you see?

I'm wild to be born, man.
I'll never be free.
Wild to be born, man.
It wasn't up to me.

GOVERNMENT ASSASSIN

Government assassin Justin Dee
Rides an old GS 550 E
Although it is long in the tooth
The engine it is bullet proof
It made him less conspicuous
Something flashy would be ridiculous
He did his work undercover
As his victims would soon discover
Government assassin Justin Dee
Rides an old GS 550 E

THE BOOK

I had a book once
It was green in colour
And thick in content
With lots of pages
And many illustrations

When I travelled, my book went with me
It fitted easily into my double-breasted leather jacket
The book became my constant companion
When I became tired and weary
My book became an excellent pillow

In times of adversity, my book became a weapon
It slew many an opponent
I would wield it loftily
And proclaim proudly
'This is my book; it has many pages'

This is my book; it has many pages.

The book

BE PROUD

Man, be proud.
Ride your motorcycle
like a knight would ride his steed.
Be cautious to other road users.
Watch out for cars pulling out.
Don't be a fool on the road.
Be cool on the road.
Be vigilant, man,
Be proud.

INDEX – FIRST LINES

Notes

Notes

Notes

Notes